# Table of Contents

# Introduction

Congratulations on downloading the book *Blockchain* and thank you for doing so.

The following chapters will discuss blockchain technology. At the end of this book, you will have enough knowledge to know how to use blockchain to better benefit you.

This book will cover everything you need to know about the blockchain platforms, cryptocurrency, and how you can use it more efficiently.

There are plenty of books on this subject on the market, thanks again for choosing this one! Every effort was made to ensure it is full of as much useful information as possible; please enjoy!

# Chapter One: What is Blockchain?

Blockchain is a list of transactions that grows every day. The blocks on the blockchain are tied to each transaction that is completed on a cryptocurrency platform such as Ethereum and Bitcoin. Each block consists of a hash pointer that can be connected to the previous block. A time stamp is stamped on each transaction so any user looking at the ledger can tell when the transaction was accepted to the chain.

The first secure blockchain happened in the early 1990s – thanks to Stuart Haber and W. Scott Stornetta. Both men were students working with a *Merkle tree*, so they could determine if they could find a more efficient way to collect data from a block.

One of the first distributions for blockchain was conceptualized by Satoshi Nakamoto in 2008 when they were working with the core components for the public ledger that is linked to Bitcoin. Blockchain tie to peer-to-peer networks that can be distributed through a server after a stamp has been placed on the transaction.

The blockchain database is managed autonomously. So, while you are using blockchain for cryptocurrencies, you will be given the guarantee that there will not be any double spending occurring unless you or an administrator grants permission for it to happen.

Nakamoto was the first to coin the term blockchain in a paper published in 2008; from there the term went on to describe all of the cryptocurrency platforms developed. In 2014, Bitcoin's blockchain file was 20 GB; the latest record is now over 100 GB.

Blockchain 2.0 was the term used when describing the new application that would take place on the distributed database. It also described a language that can be used to program smart contracts that are used by other users. After a smart contract has been written, an invoice will then be sent so that payment can be delivered after the terms of the agreement have been carried out. Blockchain 2.0 has technologies that go beyond transactions and create exchanges that end up acting as an arbiter for money and data.

When blockchain was first created, people expected it to be excluded from the global economy by allowing private protection, so people can monetize their information while being provided the capability of ensuring that the creators are paid for their intellectual property.

The second generation of blockchain made it so that a user's digital ID and personal information would be stored while providing an avenue that could aid in solving social inequality. In 2016, a new protocol was implemented so an off-chain oracle would be empowered to gain access to events and data that are not located on the network. This allows the oracle to predict the conditions for the market so the blockchain can interact with the market properly.

There are blocks that are not accepted into the chain; these blocks are called orphan blocks. Peers are built to support multiple versions of the block. The highest scoring version will be kept so that the older versions can be overwritten in the database before the data is retransmitted to their peers for improvement. There will not be anything that can guarantee the block's entry. But, it ensures that the blocks will not write over each other which can produce duplicate data.

Blockchain technology is now being used in several industries. In fact, the Russian Federation announced that they would implement a project to use blockchain technology for electronic voting. Also, the music industry uses blockchain, so royalties can be issued, and copyrights can be tracked.

### Decentralized system

If data is stored on a network, the blockchain will get rid of the risks of storing all of the information in one place. Since the blockchain is decentralized, you will need to use ad hoc messages on the distributed network.

A blockchain's network does not have the vulnerable points that hackers exploit in a centralized system. The security for blockchain includes public key cryptography. Public keys are a string of random letters and numbers that can identify every user on the network. A public key is sent to anyone who is sending coins to your wallet. The value tokens that are sent across the blockchain network will record everything tied to the public key.

Private keys, on the other hand, contain a password that users can use to access their assets that other people will not have access to. You have to keep your private key to yourself, because, if someone else has it, they can gain access to your digital currency and any other assets that are in your cryptocurrency wallet.

You may think of your public and private key as your bank account and the pin number. Your account number will be the public key that you give to someone if they want to send you money. But, the pin number will be private because it grants you access to your money.

Centralized systems will be controlled by a central authority and may experience data manipulation. However, when a system is decentralized, it will be made to where every person on the network can access the data that is there so there is nothing that can be hidden from the users.

Each node on the blockchain system will hold a copy of the blockchain. The quality of the data is maintained by the database and a computational trust. There will not be a centralized copy that exists which means no one is trusted more than someone else. Transactions will be broadcast on the network for everyone to see. These messages are sent out on a best effort basis. Mining nodes will work to validate the transaction and create blocks before the broadcast is sent from the block to the node. There are timestamp schemes that the blockchain uses so changes can be serialized by the system. Blockchain will also use proof of stake and evidence of burn.

Blockchain is constantly growing, but it carries a risk of node centralization since computers have resources that are needed when working with larger data files.

### Land registration

Blockchain has been working to create a framework in an effort to stop arguments over land ownership. A trial took place with the Sweden land registry to show how the blockchain framework would be able to speed up land sale deals. It was also used in the Republic of Georgia where blockchain was being used when creating a property registry.

### Big Four

Blockchain has four accounting firms that have been testing blockchain so other companies can examine how blockchain will help their business so that it can run more efficiently in hopes that more businesses will pick up blockchain technology. Ernst and Young is one of the companies that have been using blockchain technology by paying their employees in cryptocurrency. They even placed a Bitcoin ATM in their office, so their employees can pull cash out of their digital wallet.

The other three companies that are using blockchain technology are PwC, KPMG, and Deloitte.

## *Commercial offerings*

1. The technical university in Munich published a paper that stated how blockchain had disrupted a wide variety of industries. This study showed how venture funding caused $1.75 million to be handed over to startups in the financial sector along with those in communication and insurance. Many startups have been funded in Canada, the United States, and the United Kingdom.

2. Safe Share created an insurance blockchain that was later underwritten by Lloyd's of London.

3. Microsoft Visual Studio developed an application that worked with the Ethereum solidity language.

4. ABN Amro started a real estate project to keep track of transactions so deals could be closed faster. Another project they created is in partnership with Port of Rotterdam where a logistic tool that uses blockchain for real estate dealings.

5. QED put together a team that worked with zero knowledge blockchains. A zero-knowledge blockchain has all of the benefits that are needed for an effective party and uses a nondate disclosure for business motives.

6. The Switzerland stock exchange along with the Zurich Cantonal bank use blockchain for asset trading with the Ethereum blockchain.

7. IBM declared there would be a cloud blockchain that could be used. This cloud was given the name Hyper Ledger Fabric.

8. In 2016, Project CousenSys was founded by ConsenSys and Deloitte. This project was the creation of a digital bank that worked with blockchain cryptocurrencies.

# Chapter Two: Blockchain Technology

### *Blockchain hard forks*

A hard fork refers to an event when two blockchains split into two strings because of a rule that is set to govern the system. Take, for instance, Ethereum hard forked, so a DAO could be used with their investors. This DAO was hacked because of a vulnerability in the code. In 2014, NXT was asked to create a hard fork after a rollback on the blockchain records in an effort to mitigate the effects of a theft that resulted in $50 million being stolen. The hard fork ended up being rejected, and almost all of the funds were recovered after negotiations.

### *System openness*

When a blockchain is open, it will be user-friendly and accepted better than traditional ownership records. Traditional records may be open to the public, but they will require physical access to the documents. The first blockchains did not need permission to join which caused controversy over the definition of the term blockchain. Because of this, a debate started over if a private system needed to verify tasks while still being authorized by a central authority.

The proponents of a permissioned chain argue that the term blockchain can be applied to any structure that collects data on a block as long as there is a time stamp. Blockchains will usually serve as distributed versions of multi-version concurrency control.

There are other multi-version concurrency controls that will hold two transactions from a single object in the database. Therefore, you will have the proper opponents stated on a permissioned system, so it can begin to resemble a traditional corporate database. But, these databases do not support the verification of data like a decentralized system will. So, it will cause the system to not harden to the operator modifications.

Harvard business review defined blockchains as ledgers and databases that can be used by anyone.

### *Databases without permissions*

A significant advantage to blockchain s that it will not require permissions. Since it is open, it will be guarded against any adverse actors. In other words, the blockchain application will be added to the network, and there is not going to be anyone that has to be trusted as long as the transport layer is being used with the blockchain.

Bitcoin and other cryptocurrencies secure their blockchain with new entries that have to use proof of work. In an effort to prolong blockchain, Bitcoin uses has cash puzzles that were created by Adam Beck in the 90's.

There are still financial companies that choose not to use a decentralized blockchain in their day to day business. Venture capital was created in 2016 that was weak in the United States and strong in China. In 2017 Bitcoin was marked as the cryptocurrency that had the highest market cap out of every cryptocurrency on the market.

## Permissioned blockchains

When a blockchain holds permissions, it will have a control layer that is governed by a password to make sure that only the people who are supposed to be on it are on it. This is different from a public chain because the validators on a private chain will be vetted by an owner. Permissioned blockchains will not rely on an anonymous node to validate transactions. The New York Times stated that several corporations have been using blockchains on independent networks.

## Disadvantages to blockchain

You will see a set of adverse implications that happened during the financial crisis during 2007 and 2008 because several politically powerful actors came up with the decisions that caused the entire economy to be affected. On top of that, the blockchain will be protected through a mining effort; this means that most private blockchains will have records that an expensive computer safeguards.

## Blockchain applications

When blockchain was created, it provided new opportunities for businesses, so they could change their business models; the ledger is not going to be more than foundational technology that brought out the ability to create a new foundation without the technology being disrupted. Using disruptive technology means that there will be an attack on traditional business models that contain lower cost solutions that could overtake incumbent firms. But, some operational products will mature because of the proof of concept. While you use blockchain, you will have the guarantee of working with efficiencies that are used with asset ledgers, decentralized social networks, global supply chains, and even financial transactions.

In 2016, the blockchain skeptics spoke out. One of the people that spoke out stated that the technology for blockchain was overexaggerated while it held on to unrealistic claims, so more people would join the network. To mitigate the risks, there have been various businesses that have not wanted to invest with blockchain because they believe it will change the core of their business structure.

Blockchain's technology has been integrated into an assortment of sectors across the world. Therefore, blockchain applications will be given a disruptive innovation title because they are providing a lower cost solution that disrupts business models that are currently in place. Blockchain's protocols have been facilitated and are making it to where a business can use the new methods for processing a digital transaction. If you think about payment systems, think about the ones that promote crowd sales using cryptocurrencies.

Blockchains are automatic notarized ledgers that can take away the need for a service provider and will create less capital that can be tied into disputes. There has been a reduction in systemic risks and financial fraud because of the blockchain. You will be able to trace this decrease back to the automated process that the blockchain uses in an effort to get rid of manual work that takes up time that may be used in other business processes. In the end, it comes down to the blockchain being able to be used for a wide range of tasks such as collecting taxes.

The new distribution methods will be open when you work in the insurance sector. There are some banks that have shown an interest in blockchain technology, so they can speed up settlements. IoT and sharing economy is a benefit that is used by the blockchain and other collaborating peers.

# Chapter Three: Blockchain Benefits

Blockchain will offer you advantages that you will not find anywhere else. There are disadvantages to using blockchain, but by focusing on the benefits, you will get closer to investing with blockchain.

Using blockchain will not be like traditional trading because you will have other options of trading such as mining cryptocurrency, buying cryptocurrency, and selling cryptocurrency.

Blockchain allows for your identity to be protected because there is no reason for you to put your personal information into the system. Therefore, your name, credit card number, and email never have to be placed on the blockchain thus making it safer for you to use. You will not have to worry about your identity being hacked, the biggest thing you have to worry about is protecting your private key so that your cryptocurrencies are kept safe.

Your email will be changed each time you create a transaction which means you never have to use your personal email. So, you will not receive an email from blockchain when you complete a transaction.

When it comes sending payments, you will not have a processing fee to pay. And, if you are sending money overseas, there will not be a transaction fee. This is helpful especially when you are traveling abroad and using cryptocurrency because you will not have to pay a fee to exchange your money.

# Chapter Four: The Future of Blockchain

There is no telling what will happen with blockchain because no one can tell the future. You can, however, make predictions on what could happen based on what blockchain is currently doing.

The truth is that blockchain is like any other piece of technology that comes out, it will have its ups and downs, and there will be times when people wonder if it is worth the effort to continue investing with blockchain; especially when the cryptocurrency market is down. But, you may want to keep investing with blockchain because it is still new.

For the first few years, most new technology does well, but after that, no one knows what will happen. With how blockchain has been doing and with how many cryptocurrencies are being developed and distributed every day. The prediction that blockchain will be around for many years to come from looking at the companies and governments that have been investing with blockchain around the world as well as the businesses that are creating their own blockchains to conduct business.

But, like any investments, you need to be careful when investing with blockchain because there will not be any way to know if you will make a profit or not. Investing with blockchain will mean you are putting yourself at risk for the system to crash and for everyone on that system to lose the cryptocurrency that is in their wallet. This may not seem like something that will happen; it is a possibility.

You will never know the future of blockchain unless you keep up with the news and any new articles that come out about blockchain, so you can anticipate changes that may be coming. The better you can predict what blockchain can do, the easier it will be for you to use it.

## Chapter Five: Changes in the Financial Sector Because of Blockchain

When blockchain was created, it was created to bring solutions for startup ventures that had been denied by the traditional financial industry. Blockchain supports cryptocurrency and helps with the cryptocurrencies that banks cannot offer. Blockchain also allows you to track your financial assets in a secure environment while reducing the risk of being hacked or your data being modified without your permission. On top that, the complexity of how a transaction is carried out will be reduced because of blockchain.

Blockchain also makes it easier for you to manage the digital risks that come with the financial industry. Ledgers can be created to send out the information to the people needing the information. However, if someone does not need access to the data, it will not be given to them which means that your data can be kept safe from any competitors that you have. Blockchain gets rid of the need to print out paperwork and the process required to ensure that everyone has the paperwork required. Therefore, no one will have the ability to say they lost the paperwork because they can instantly pull the paperwork up on their computer to take note of the details laid out in the contract.

In 2012, Bitcoin rose to the top of its industry with over a billion dollars being transferred through the system. In every year that has followed, more people have been using blockchain, therefore, moving more money safely through the system. Companies all over the world have been using blockchain in an effort to get into the coin market as well as improve the services that they offer their customers so that their banking experience is better than it has been. But, not every bank is eager to jump on the blockchain bandwagon because they are afraid that it will eliminate the services that they already offer their customers. However, this is not true. If anything, blockchain will improve the services that they have to offer, so their customers continue to come back to their bank.

With technology on what seems like a daily basis, the fees that are attached to most banking experiences will be reduced. With more risks being reduced, the time that people used to have to sit and deal with the risks has been opened up, so they can accomplish more in a day! Any payment going through the system will have the default setting of being premeditated, so there does not have to be duplicate documentation for that payment.

The financial institutions that have been using blockchain have created teams inside their branches to offer help to customers with any need they may have when it comes to starting a business with blockchain.

One of the best things about blockchain is that some of the common mistakes made in the financial industry will be reduced because blockchain can handle payments and any documents that are placed on a block will be living documents so that users can look at payments that have been made or need to be made. This will make it to where users can ensure they have everything in line, so their payment is in on time and there are not any late fees being tied to the user's account. Not only that, but users will no longer have to rely on their memory to make sure that they are paying on time.

Startup companies will be required to provide accurate projections for their business before they can acquire the funding that they need. This will provide banks an accurate depiction of how the business will do as it grows. By seeing these projections, the bank will no longer be risking money on a company that cannot pay it back because it does not survive past its first year. So, the money that was being given to the companies that have not survived can be given to those that can!

# Chapter Six: How Blockchain Works with Cryptocurrency

Cryptocurrency is known as a crypto asset that can be traded across the blockchain platform through secure transactions. Digital currency will come in the form of value tokens like Bitcoin or Ether (there are thousands of other value tokens that you can trade across the blockchain platform) . As the years have passed since Bitcoin cryptocurrency has grown and other cryptocurrencies have come and passed. But, the two that you will hear about the most are still around, and those are Bitcoin and Ether.

Cryptocurrencies are similar to blockchain because they are a decentralized system which means that there will be a chain of all the transactions completed which will result in a block being created for that transaction. Every transaction will have its own block. This means that cryptocurrency will not be like traditional banking systems. Cryptocurrency will work on an anonymous electronic cash system that was first introduced in 1998 with the cryptocurrency known as B-money. After that, Bit gold was created, and finally, Bitcoin came around. The issues that users had with B-money and Bit gold were fixed when the two cryptocurrencies were combined and published for the public to use.

The Nakamoto identity created Bitcoin with a hash function that is used by Bitcoin users. In 2011, Namecoin was developed while trying to help the DNS decentralization of the system. However, the internet censorship group ended up coming down hard on Namecoin, and ultimately it was shut down. Litecoin was released shortly after Namecoin as the first cryptocurrency to use a hash function outside of Bitcoin. Later on, Peercoin was developed as a hybrid currency that uses proof of work and proof of steak to verify the transactions on its system.

While you are looking for a cryptocurrency to use, you will discover that there are different programs that you can use. But, there are programs that have been shut down because they were not as successful as Bitcoin or Ethereum. In 2014, the United Kingdom's Department of Treasury conducted a study, so they could observe how cryptocurrency would change their economy.

Around the same period of time, the second generation of cryptocurrency programs was released for the public to use. There have been some programs like Ethereum and NXT that use advanced functions so that users can use a stealth address or smart contracts.

Cryptocurrency has also threatened the price of financial institutes. With cryptocurrencies being secure and easier to use, there is more trading occurring on blockchain which has caused customers to lose faith in fiat currency that they have been using their entire lives. Thanks to the widespread use of cryptocurrency, it has become difficult for financial institutions to obtain the information that they need to observe what the economy is doing, which is done so the government can sway it in the direction they want it to go in.

## Chapter Seven: Implementing Blockchain So It Can Benefit You

Knowing the purpose behind blockchain will determine how far you need to go so you can invest at the level you want. Blockchain can be used by a company or by individuals; the majority of people use individual accounts.

Using blockchain as an individual means that you have to set up a cryptocurrency wallet, so your coins are kept safe. Your wallet can run off your computer or your mobile devices. In all honesty, digital wallets are safer than physical wallets because they cannot be left someone and stolen. On top of that, they are harder to be hacked.

A software wallet will require a third-party service so the wallet can be downloaded to your computer. Once the wallet has been downloaded to your hard drive, you will have access to every transaction you make at your fingertips.

After you have gotten your wallet, you will need to pick your cryptocurrency. Cryptocurrency can be traded for good and services that are offered through the blockchain platform and even through businesses. Not every business will allow you to pay in cryptocurrency, but those that do are paving a path for the ones that follow. If you do not want to use your coins to purchase something, then you may use them to trade with someone. However, finding someone to trade with could be difficult because most people want to hold onto their cryptocurrency and let it grow in value.

Bitcoins and any other cryptocurrency can be bought or traded on a cryptocurrency exchange. These coins can be purchased with a different value token, or they can be obtained with a fiat currency.

Blockchain allows programs to be run through your computer's CPU so that coins can be mined. But, your CPU will need to be high-grade to do this. And, as the blockchain platform evolves, you may see that CPU mining can no longer be done and you will only be able to mine if you have a mining rig.

## Chapter Eight: Revealing the Truth About Blockchain Myths

When people do not understand blockchain, they make up information in an attempt to understand it better. But, the data that they are placing out there for other people to see is wrong, and you will discover the myths people have made up about Bitcoin and what the truth is.

The database for blockchain is constantly growing. Even though blockchain is a distributed network, there is not a single computer that holds the entire chain. Therefore, instead of participating nodes will have a copy of the string. Because of the transactions that are constantly added to the blockchain database, the nodes are constantly needing to be updated. Blockchain has two elements that help run it.

1. The transactions that are created because of the participants in the system.

2. The records on the blocks that are keeping track of transactions, so they are placed in the correct sequence and are not being tampered with.

The most significant advantage that blockchain has going for it is that it is open to the public. Since anyone can participate in the blockchain networks and see the blocks as well as the contents of the block, this does not mean they will have the option of seeing the content of the transaction that has been completed by someone else, and that is because of the user's private key. Since blockchain is decentralized, there will not be a central authority accepting your transactions. So, there will be a lot of trusts placed on those that participate in the network. But, the biggest advantage for blockchain is how secure it is. The database can be extended, but it can never be changed.

If you want to add a transaction to the chain, then other users will need o verify it. The verification process consists of an algorithm that has to be completed so the transaction can be validated. The term valid will mean something different on each blockchain. The approved transactions will be placed on a block, and that block will be sent to the nodes on the network to create a new block. Every block will consist of its own hash or have its own fingerprint to make it unique. Blockchain will ensure that none of the data can be modified without there being a timestamped layer that will remove several layers of human checking and then will cause the transaction to be immutable. There are three types of blockchains that you can use.

1. Federated: these blockchains will participate in a consensus process. They will have a limited number of nodes that will be granted permission to complete tasks. These blockchains are usually saved for pharmaceutical companies or government entities.
2. Private: a private blockchain will be the blockchain a company uses while allowing specific members to carry out tasks.
3. Public: this is the blockchain that is used by everyone. Each user can see the transactions that are completed once they have been placed on the public ledger.

Myth 1: blockchain is a database located in the cloud.

Blockchain is a flat file that will record transactions. The transaction list will append the entries that cannot be removed thus causing the database to grow as it replicates a peer to peer network. Blockchain will not allow any physical information to be stored in the string such as a word document. The chain will provide proof of existence in a distributed ledger that will contain code to verify the presence of a report without verifying the actual report. Then the file will be stored in a data lake where only the owner will have access to it.

Myth 2: blockchain will change the world.

Blockchain is making complex transactions more comfortable, but it is hard to say if blockchain will change the world or not. This is because blockchain will not have the ability to get rid of online fraud and users will always be skeptical of the confidentiality that blockchain offers.

Myth 3: blockchain is free

Blockchain is not entirely free. There are several computers that are being used to solve algorithms to produce a final result which will eventually become the single version of the truth. Every block will use a significant amount of computing power so the algorithm can be solved. Therefore, someone will need to pay for the computing power that is used to support the blockchain services.

Myth 4: there is only one blockchain

There are various versions of blockchain because there is a blockchain platform for every cryptocurrency that is developed.

Myth 5: blockchain can be used for everything.

The code behind blockchain is power, but it cannot create miracles. This means that it cannot solve all of the world's problems. Most of what blockchain will be used for is tied to math instead of being tied to the law.

Myth 6: blockchain will be the backbone of the global economy.

This cannot be done because a central entity does not own blockchain. For this reason, there will always be people who believe that using a private blockchain will get them support from at least a dozen cryptocurrencies. It has been reported that blockchain's network is comparable to the NASDAQ network.

Myth 7: the ledger on blockchain is locked and cannot be unlocked.

The larger transactions will be similar to bank records which means that they are private and can be linked to a specific institute. Even though the blockchain is public, the transactions have to be verified and placed on the network cryptographically. If there is any fraudulent activity found on the blockchain, the transaction will be rejected in an attempt to prevent fraud. Since mining is one of the most prominent financial incentives, it is believed that it will rewrite historical transactions. But, for the time being, the computational resources are being improved over time.

Myth 8: blockchain records cannot be hacked or altered

While this is true, there are some exceptional hackers that can get through blockchain's security and into the system. But, they will be caught before they can alter any of the records.

Myth 9: blockchain will only be used in the financial sector.

If you follow blockchain, then you know this is not true. Blockchain is used by the government, insurance agencies, health care providers, real estate, and even on a personal level as well.

Myth 10: blockchain is Bitcoin.

Bitcoin has its own blockchain, but it does not make up the entire blockchain. Every cryptocurrency has its own blockchain. One way Bitcoin has been described is as "a cryptocurrency that makes electronic payments possible directly between two people without going through a third party like a bank."

Myth 11: blockchain is only for business transactions

Blockchain was created to change the global economy as the dot-coms did in the 90s. That does not mean that it is only open for big companies to use, anyone, can use it! The only exception is that the user has to have an internet connection.

# Chapter Nine: How to Start Investing in Blockchain

A wide assortment of business models has been transformed because of blockchain. When you look at blockchain, you will notice that it is similar to an Excel spreadsheet that is work done by every member of an organization. This "digital spreadsheet" operates on a decentralized network.

Because of how blockchain is written, it consists of unique factors that you may not be able to understand. Blockchain does not follow the same path as traditional trading because there are several levels that are used when a user logs onto the system.

There are at least five ways you can create an investment with blockchain and cryptocurrency that will benefit you later on down the road.

1. Stockpiling coins

A lot of investors stockpile gold so they can sell it when the price goes up. But, there are other investors that have begun to stockpile cryptocurrency. Stockpiling gold and cryptocurrency have their advantages and disadvantages when it comes to supply and demand. When the supply is limited, then the demand will go up. And, when the demand goes up, the value increases which will provide the perfect time for an investor to sell what they are stockpiling.

2. Penny stocks

Penny stocks are cryptocurrency like Bitcoin, but they work on a different system because they are competing with Bitcoin. You should think of cryptocurrency like gold. It is a rare commodity and should be treated as such.

3. Crowdfunding

Crowdfunding is a method that can be used when you are attempting to raise capital. The coins will not need to be used when you are dealing with crowdfunding. Instead, coins will be given to you by investors before you start mining. This is usually done before the system becomes open to the public.

4. Angel funding and startup ventures

Blockchain has made it possible for entrepreneurs and investors to come together and get the funding that they need for their business. Whenever you use angel funding, you will be using a form of crowdfunding so you can obtain the money that you need. On top of that, you will have the opportunity to find an investor for your company! The investors that are located on blockchain will be different from any investors that are found through traditional means.

5. Pure blockchain technology

Blockchain's technology is on the rise, and there are companies that are trying to take advantage of it by using it and getting their names out there. One company called Global Arena Holdings uses blockchain technology as leverage, so their votes are verified.

# Chapter Ten: Blockchain Terms You Should Know

There are some terms you will hear when you are using blockchain that you do not understand or you know but you do not know the blockchain definition of it. Here you can learn how blockchain defines every word that you will hear when using it.

1. Address: where you will send and receive transactions on the blockchain network. Your address will be a string of alphanumeric characters and a scannable QR code. The Bitcoin address is similar to a set of keys. One key will be known to the public because that is where your transactions occur, and the other will be your private key that allows you to get into your account.

2. Bitcoin ATM: this is similar to a regular ATM in the respect that it is a physical machine,but you can purchase Bitcoins with cash. You may also hear a Bitcoin ATM called BTM or Bitcoin AVM.

3. Bitcoin price index (BPI): the BPI is a representation of the average price for Bitcoin across the leading global exchange. However, it will be required to meet criteria that were set by the BPI.

4. Bit pay: a payment processor used for Bitcoins. Bit pay allows merchants to take Bitcoin as payment.

5. Blockchain: a full list of blocks that have been mined since cryptocurrency started. Blockchain was designed so that every block holds a piece of the block that came before it. Blockchain is tamperproof.

6. Block reward: the reward that the miner receives for successfully completing a transaction block. The reward can be a mixture of coins and transaction fees that will follow cryptocurrency policy.

7. Client: the client will be a software program used by a computer or mobile device. The client will aid the connection between the computer or mobile device to the Bitcoin network.

8. Cryptocurrency: a form of currency based on mathematics. Cryptocurrency is not printed money and is produced by solving mathematical problems that come from cryptography.

9. Cryptography: a mathematical encryption code that will help conceal any information so it can be verified and secured.

10. Exchange: a central resource that will be used for exchanging money and digital assets.

11. Fiat currency: this is the currency that is produced by the government and holds value because people say it does. Fiat currency can be used in terrorist attacks and money laundering.

12. Hash: a mathematical process that takes the variable amount of data that is given to produce a shorter outcome. The hashing function has two fundamental characteristics. The first is that it is mathematically challenging to work out what the original input was just by looking at the output. The second, a challenging part of the input will provide you with an entirely different result.

13. Hash rate: how many hashes a miner can produce in a specific amount of time.

14. Input: the payment that comes from the transaction. Most of the time the Bitcoin address will be the input unless a trade provides one. In other words, unless the Bitcoin is mined, then the input will be a Bitcoin address.

15. KYC: know your client or customer

16. Mining: the act of generating new Bitcoins. This process will be completed by solving cryptographic problems with computer hardware.

17. Node: any computer connected to the Bitcoin network will have their transactions sent through the nodes.

18. Output: the destination for the transaction. One operation can produce multiple outputs.

19. Pre-mining: a coin can be mined before the cryptocurrency has been released. Pre-mining is a standard technique that scam coins will use, but the coins that use pre-mining are not always scam coins. Ensure you are doing all of your research before you determine if the coin is a scam coin or not.

20. Private key: a key kept secret by the users. When the private key is used it acts as a digital signature when hashed with a public key.

21. Proof of work: a system that ties the mining capability to computation power. Blocks will need to be hashed by a natural computational process. However, there will be an added variable that has to be added to the process that will make it more difficult. After a block has been hashed successfully, then the hashing will be the proof of work needed to get the block validated.

22. Public key: the key that is publicly known as a hashed block.

23. Scam coin: an altcoin that is produced to make money for the person who created the coin. You may see these coins appear in pre-mining situations.

24. Transaction fee: a transaction fee will be imposed on various transactions that occur on the Bitcoin network. The transaction fee will be rewarded to the miner that mines the block successfully.

25. Wallet: where coins are stored. Coins can also be sent from one wallet to another.

# Chapter Eleven: Smart Contracts and Blockchain

Smart contracts are comprised of computer code that is activated after the blockchain has registered a predetermined incident. Smart contracts will be given their own block and distributed as part of the blockchain chain.

It may appear to be complicated, but you can also think of smart contracts in the same manner that you would think of functions on your checking account. Many checking accounts have automated deductions that can be set up by the user or a third-party as long as they have the user's permission. A smart contract will work in a similar manner only from a decentralized position. In other words, smart contracts are a computer's equivalent of the legalese in a contract that stipulates how all of the details are carried and when it will happen.

On top of that, if a smart contract is generated on a public blockchain then, there will not be any third party who has the option of setting in and actively preventing the transaction from being carried out. The transaction will be equally secure as long as it is performed by a blockchain platform. This is due to the extreme type of security that has been built into the blockchain model.

What's more, smart contracts that are executed through a blockchain are open for anyone to see as long as they have a copy of the string. This means that a smart contract will never be open for debate or discussion since it is an expression of the facts as they have been stated. This could be a miracle or a curse depending on what information has been made public.

Any smart contract where computer protocol can carry out, verify, and enforce the negotiation will get rid of the need for any agreement with a contractual clause.

Smart contracts will contain a user interface that will emulate the logic of contractual clause(s). The proponents of a smart contract will claim that various contractual clauses can be made partial or entirely self-executing or self-enforcing.

A smart contract will aim to provide security that is above any traditional contract that has to be executed by the law. Therefore, smart contracts will reduce transaction fees that are tied to the process of drawing a deal.

*Common uses for smart contracts*

Since market penetration is rising for various financial technologies, smart contracts have become more prevalent. One of the biggest reasons is because smart contracts are simplifying many common contract usage cases. Take, for instance; smart contracts have made it easier for users to update their contract terms in real time instead of having wait days for a physical copy to be sent back and forth to both parties. This helps with the speed of the process, but it also increases the odds of their accuracy remaining at an acceptable level.

Smart contracts will require fewer resources to be used to the fullest. Even though this does not make a lot of sense to people who do not use smart contracts frequently, when they are used for business transactions, the savings will be substantial. Because of the guarantee and the safe nature of smart contracts, this means that the contract can be executed without a third party needing to be involved. Financial institutions will discover that smart contracts can help improve their business in numerous ways. When it comes to trade clearing or settlements, the final result will result in settlements, transfers, and trades being tailored for the users. A smart contract can also be used when dealing with coupon payments, specifically the returned principal on expired bonds. Smart contracts can also be used with insurance claims, so errors are minimized, and the flow of work is streamlined between departments. Lastly, they are known for improving the regulation of IoT services.

The healthcare industry can also use smart contracts! Smart contracts are being used to improve the accuracy for when medical records are updated and when patients are transferred between departments. They can also be used in monitoring the health of the population through a public blockchain that refreshes automatically while paying participants for using their information. Smart contracts are already being used with IoT devices that help determine the success of fitness goals and release rewards accordingly.

When looking at the music industry smart contracts are being used to track royalties for song usage and distributing payments. It can also be put to use on a smaller scale, so interactions between two people are improved while predicting things like trade energy credits as well as increased peer lending opportunities. This will be the same technology that is being used for the Tesla electric car, where users can charge at a charging station and be billed for the transaction instantly.

Smart contracts are also changing how products are shipped and tracked by sending the documentation while various production pieces make their way through processing and shipping. This may even be cued for the input of signatures which means that the process will be seamless for signing a contract to receive goods. That way, if there are questions about the quality of the shipment,then the entire route can be tracked from beginning to end.

Credit enforcement has made smart contracts an extension of property law. Credit agreements will disable the product that has been purchased if you do not make the payments that you agree to make. For example, you get a new car on credit, but you do not make your payment. The doors will lock the vehicle will drive itself back to the dealership.

But,with electrical products, there will be a kill switch that can be disabled as long as the conditions are met by both parties. This will happen as long as payments are made through a public channel such as Bitcoin.

# Chapter Twelve: The Ethereum Platform

Ethereum is one of many blockchain platforms that are public and has a programmable transaction functionality. In simpler terms, Ethereum decentralizes and provides a peer to peer contract by using a value token known as Ether. Ethereum was proposed by Vitalik Buterin in 2013. But, the next generation of cryptocurrency and its decentralized application platform were not funded and developed until the following year.

Buterin was a programmer that worked on Bitcoin and wanted to provide a platform that solved all the issues Bitcoin had. Instead of using the Bitcoin protocol,Ethereum creates its own blockchain to provide higher developmental flexibility.It accomplishes this by using the Turing programming language.

While Ethereum was being developed, the developers said that it would extend the blockchain beyond the peer to peer system. Like any other project, there were questions that arose about the security and scalability of the program. Despite all that, Buterin received the World Technology Award in 2014.

July 30, 2015, the blockchain went live. At first, the program was developed by Ethereum Switzerland GmbH and the Ethereum foundation. But, when the spring of 2016 came around, the ether value token was worth more than one billion dollars. Voxnoted that the new digital currency would be a challenge to Bitcoin because it was able to provide a different range of services that Bitcoin could not provide.

*Ether*

Ether is the value token associated with the Ethereum blockchain. It will be stored in your wallet just like Bitcoins are.

*Pros and cons*

There are pros and cons to using Ethereum. Below you will see the pros first and then the cons of the system.

1.  Contracts are enforced as they are written.

Contracts will always be executed as they are written. Whenever a contract is written, it sometimes has to be enforced by a judge or a lawyer which can be an extremely expensive process for everyone involved. But, with the DAO (Distributed Autonomous Organization) people are going to great lengths to ensure their contracts are written properly before they can be enforced because the contract has to operate within the confines of the DAO.

Because of this, there is no longer the need to involve judges and lawyers. Therefore, you will be saving money. While Ethereum continues to adapt and strengthen, there will be more things like this introduced into the wonderful world of technology.

 2.  Crowdales and DAOs.

Ethereum and a DAO called Digix were both crowdfunded by a digital currency known ad Dapp. The funding for Digix was raised in a short period of time, and it was raised entirely by ether!

 3.  Automation and little to no cost

Since Ethereum is based on a DAO, there is the possibility that it could be designed at zero cost because of the business functions that are executed automatically. But, because of the price of gas that is tied to the implementing of smart contracts, you will find that there is a small cost that is associated with running a DAO. However, these costs are minimal compared to the cost of having to have an office. Looking at EtherEx, you will notice that they tried to set up a decentralized and trustless cryptocurrency that could be copied over to the EtherEx foundation. This foundation has an infrastructure that votes on important decisions such as how coins will be distributed and how to help with the cost of gas.

Since most businesses are built inside the Ethereum DAO, the cost is constantly being reduced when it comes to setting up a business when a building is not required. Everything will be done through technology and can be done anywhere in the world. The cost of gas will be smaller than having to pay employees to come into an office every day.

Now here are some of the cons for Ethereum.

 1.  Still new

Ethereum is still new which means that it is still being developed as it continues to grow. With Ethereum trying to bypass Bitcoin in operations that it allows, it will have to be shut down from time to time to make sure that it is still updated properly.

2. Lawyers

Taking lawyers and judges out of the equation may be a good thing, but it can also lead to problems since people will have to make informed decisions. Computers are great, but they will always require a human to make sure that the coding and functionality are running as it should.

3. Change

Change is not always a bad thing, but when you are on a deadline, and you cannot finish your work because the system shut down, then it is a disadvantage that could turn you off the platform.

4. The bandwagon

With Ethereum still being new, there is the possibility that people will jump on it and go with it which means that there will not be as many blocks that have to be mined or no one will get on it, and you will be left doing all the work and possibly losing all the oceans that you get because the platform could not succeed.

Despite the fact that there are negatives to Ethereum, that does not mean that you should not look at it as a blockchain that you could use. The Ethereum blockchain will provide you with a lot of great opportunities that Bitcoin cannot provide you.

# Chapter Thirteen: The Bitcoin Platform

Blockchain means that there are public records that have been used when creating new blocks. But, the best solution is not to be forcing a central authority into the system that can be trusted to make decisions since these decisions cannot be made with the power a central authority would have. Maintenance on the chain will be completed by the network through software that the chain uses to run on a regular basis. In simpler terms, an alive person does not have to run the blockchain which makes sit to where human error is decreased.

The network will see be used with validating negotiations that are done so that they can be added to the ledger once the node has been marked as available for broadcasting when the consultation is completed. Given the proper verification, Bitcoin will take the data and distribute it to where it needs to be. Therefore, each node that is used will start a new chain in the blockchain for every negotiation that a miner completes.

A new block is created six times every hour or when a negotiation has been accepted and verified. Bitcoin's software will aid in figuring out how much is owed by the miner, so the amount is not sent twice without there being permission granted by the system to do so. This is an additional security measure put in place to make sure that the system does not overlook anything.

Blockchain ledgers will look at the data that has been recorded for transfers and will be in several distinct parts of the system so they can be sorted out based on the notes that are written on the negotiation or the bills that are placed in a different location on the network. The value tokens will be the only form of currency that can be spent on a block in the blockchain.

If anyone is using the blockchain to mine coins, then a new block will be created so it can be maintained until mining has been completed and the reward is sent out. Miners can obtain rewards for the transactions that they achieve after they have been verified and put on a block in the blockchain.

# Chapter Fourteen: Creating a Wallet for Blockchain

## *Software wallet*

1. Look at your options. There are several different wallets that have been created. The wallet that you choose should be based on the security and control that you have over your coins because of the software that you are using. But, a big hassle will be the fact that you have to download the software, install it, and maintain it on your own.

   a. Since blockchain is a public database, any transaction that is processed through the server will not be stored until it is verified.

2. Bitcoin Core is the original Bitcoin wallet and as Bitcoin has evolved, so has the wallet. There are people who have said good things about the wallet and some have claimed that it is one of the best wallets for you to use. To download this wallet, you will need to go to the Bitcoin wallet and download the application. Once the software has been installed, the client will establish a network and begin downloading the blockchain.

   a. You need to have all the blocks in the chain before you can complete any transaction.

3. There are other wallets that you will have the option to download, and if you do not want to use Bitcoin core, then you should look at all the pros and cons of each wallet as well as the functions that they will offer you. For example, there are some wallets that you can only get on Mac while others will only allow you to download on a Windows PC. Two things that you need to remember are:

   a. Each wallet will have its own installment quirk.

   b. The Hive wallet will be a wallet that is geared towards blockchain beginners.

4. Lightweight wallets will take up less room on your hard drive. These wallets will also work faster because they do not have to download the entire blockchain. Two of the best lightweight wallers are Electrum and Multibit.

   a. Lightweight wallets will not be as secure as wallets that have to download the entire blockchain.

## *Web wallet*

1. You need to understand a web wallet before you can use it. These wallets will take your private key and store it on a server that an admin group will control. These wallets can be linked to your mobile and software wallets as

well. You can access your wallet anywhere you want as long as you have internet access. The wallet website will oversee your public and private key and may even take coins without you knowing about it. However, this is highly unlikely.

    a. There have been a lot of web wallets that have experienced security breaches in the past. So, you need to check if the wallet you want to use has had any risks before you started looking at it.

2. When you pick your web wallet, there are a lot that of wallets that say they have tight security, so their customers feel safe using their product. A few of the most popular web wallets are Xapo, Coinnbase, and Circle.

    a. Coinbase will give you offers worldwide, and they are also an exchange service.

    b. Xapo is a simple wallet that is user-friendly and offers extra security through cold storage.

    c. Circle allows US citizens to link their bank accounts to their web wallet, so it is easier for them to deposit money. Other countries can use debit and credit cards.

3. Use a wallet that is anonymous. There are a few web wallets that offer less security and do not provide their users any insurance. The dark wallet will be an extension that can be placed on chrome and is one of the most popular anonymous wallets. The servers will fluctuate to offer you stability for your coins. But, the server may become vulnerable and could be hacked at any time.

    a. There are other anonymous wallets that have features you may find appealing such as fast cash.

## *Hardware wallet*

1. If you are overly protective of your finances, then a hardware wallet will be the best for you. These are physical devices that will have a private key and will work electronically to facilitate payments. A hardware wallet will be like the one that you carry on your person, and it will not need to rely on a third-party for storage.

    a. Hardware wallets are also immune to viruses and Trojan Horses that you may see infect software wallets.

2. There are various hardware wallets that you can buy. The quality of the wallet will depend on the price range.

    a. A Pi wallet will use cold storage and will not have any wireless capabilities that you may want to use. It will be using the Armory client to ensure that it is secure while not requiring you to set it up on your own. This is a user-friendly wallet and is safe to use as a hardware wallet.

b. USB wallets will be the most affordable and are quite popular. A USB wallet will protect that data you place on them and use a microprocessor chip that is like the chip in updated credit cards. USB hardware wallets will allow you to use several different computers with your device as long as you have a secure connection.

c. Trezor is similar to Pi, but it uses a small screen that you can interact with. There are private keys that are generated by the device, and it is also immune to malware and viruses.

3. It is wise to encrypt your wallet. Most hardware wallets will require a password or a code so it can be encrypted when you set it up. But, if your device does not require one, then you will want to go in and add one so that it is more secure. Each hardware wallet will have a different protocol that you have to follow so you can encrypt your wallet.

# Chapter Fifteen: Blockchain is Changing the World

Each chapter in this book has shown you how blockchain has changed various sectors for the better. Blockchain causes the financial industry to be more efficient and more secure so that people can keep their money secure. But, if you are looking at the financial sector, you will most likely see something about cryptocurrency because it has changed everything as we know it. While blockchain has its advantages and disadvantages, you will have to look past them to see just how blockchain has changed businesses and how customers look at those businesses.

Every transaction will have to be completed once it has been started. There are a couple of protocols that have been put in place to make sure that the ledger is correct and only holds information that is a hundred percent accurate. The data on the blockchain cannot be modified without the modification being verified. This means that the blockchain is safe from hackers or anyone that would want to hack it because they would have to hack into every computer at once and that is virtually impossible. The only thing that a hacker can get into is your account, and they will need to have your public key and your password as you saw earlier. This is why it is vital for you to ensure that your account is safe, so you do not lose everything.

When blockchain technology first came around, it was a hit thanks to the protocol that was put in place when it came to dealing with documents and digital assets that were being placed inside blocks. As the assets are transferred, a smart contract can be put into place so the process can be automated and you can make sure that everything is done without payment being sent before the work has been finished. If a smart contract is in place, then organizations will have the option to run at a cheaper rate. With more organizations becoming more affordable, then they can put the money they are saving somewhere else so they can continue to make their business more efficient for their customers.

Analysts have predicted that by 2022 blockchain will be widely accessible and could end up costing the financial industry twenty billion dollars since it has been placed on the blockchain.

With that being said, there are some industries that will get left behind, and it will push them to want to change so they can keep up with their customers and with technology; it is also a way for them ensure that they do not lose their customers.

# Chapter Sixteen: Blockchain and Businesses

The biggest downside to blockchain is that you cannot reverse a transaction once it has been made. Therefore, you will need to be cautious when you are sending coins because once it is gone, there is a possibility that you will not get a refund from the person that received the coins. Basically, make sure you are keeping a good handle on where you send your coins and add extra security to your system so your coins cannot be stolen.

Keeping your cryptocurrency will mean you have to deal with volatility. The value of cryptocurrency will fluctuate as time passes and the longer that you hold onto them, the less value they may. But, there is the possibility that the value of the coins will go up and when you sell them, then you will get more money. On the other hand, if you plan on spending the coins on good or services, then you will need to make sure you know how much the coin is worth so that you do not have to spend more than you plan to. In other words, you will be gambling with your coins the longer you keep them.

Some companies such as TigerDirect and Etsy accept cryptocurrency as a form of payment if you do not want to pay with your credit card. But, big multimillion dollar companies like Wal-Mart and Target have not gotten on board yet. And, there is no telling when they will get on board because of how well they are doing dealing with fiat currency alone. But, you may see them accepting cryptocurrency before too long because the value of certain cryptocurrency coins are going up and there are more people using them.

Cryptocurrency is similar to cash despite the fact that it is digital. There will not be any extended warranties that you have to deal with, but then again you will not get any rewards like you would if you were to use a credit card. With cryptocurrency, your policy will never change, and you will not have to deal with the fees. An added bonus is that you will not have to deal with the headache of your cryptocurrency dropping your credit score because you could not pay for it that month.

The most prominent similarity to credit cards that cryptocurrency has is that is not accepted everywhere.

When you look at the business side of it, using Bitcoins will save you money. If you use services such as Coinbase, then your first million dollars that you make accepting Bitcoins will be free. From there you will have to pay at least one percent of the transactions that are completed in your business. However, this is still less than the fee you will pay if you accept credit cards.

Exchanges that work with cryptocurrency will allow you to convert it to cash quickly without worrying about volatility. Not to mention, you do not have to worry about chargebacks or hackers stealing your customer's credit card information. The merchants that use cryptocurrency will typically work off a tablet or smartphone to accept payment. This is an added benefit because you will not need a big system that can only stay in one place. Therefore, you can take your business anywhere and accept payments which is a major plus for a lot of businesses!

# Conclusion

Thank you for making it through to the end of this book, let's hope it was informative and able to provide you with all of the tools you need to achieve your goals whatever they may be.

The next step is to choose the cryptocurrency you would like to invest with, so you can begin to use the blockchain platform. Blockchain is helpful in so many ways and is changing how people look at their money. Because of blockchain and cryptocurrencies, you will be the one in control of their money without having to worry about a third-party being involved.

We hope by now you understand how blockchain works and how using it will benefit you in the long run.

This book does not have all of the information that you could possibly want to know about blockchain, but it is a great start. We encourage you to do more research. Make sure that you do not start investing until you feel comfortable with the knowledge that you have.

If you need more information, you might want to connect to groups or people in social media and forums that are experienced in using blockchain. Do not be afraid to reach them out and ask for assistance. Doing so will help you grow your understanding about this complex technology.

Finally, if you found this book useful in any way, a review on Amazon is always appreciated!

Thank you and good luck!

www.ingramcontent.com/pod-product-compliance
Lightning Source LLC
Chambersburg PA
CBHW071158220526
45468CB00003B/1070